The Oregon Trail

by Jean F. Blashfield

Content Adviser: Professor Sherry L. Field,
Department of Social Science Education,
College of Education, The University of Georgia

Reading Adviser: Dr. Linda D. Labbo,
Department of Reading Education,
College of Education, The University of Georgia

COMPASS POINT BOOKS

Minneapolis, Minnesota

Compass Point Books
3722 West 50th Street, #115
Minneapolis, MN 55410

Visit Compass Point Books on the internet at *www.compasspointbooks.com* or e-mail your request
to *custserv@compasspointbooks.com*

Photographs ©: FPG International/G. Randall, cover; Visuals Unlimited/Don W. Fawcett, 5; North
Wind Picture Archives, 6; Wyoming Division of Cultural Resources, 7; Missouri Historical
Society, St. Louis, 9 top; Kansas State Historical Society, 9 bottom; Missouri Historical Society,
St. Louis, 10 top; Oregon Historical Society, 10 bottom; North Wind Picture Archives, 11; Stock
Montage, Inc., 12; Corbis, 13; Corbis/Dave Bartruff, 14; FPG International/Ed Cooper, 19;
Wyoming Division of Cultural Resources, 20; North Wind Picture Archives, 22; Visuals
Unlimited/Ron Spomer, 24; Nebraska State Historical Society, 25; Visuals Unlimited/Preston J.
Garrrison, 27; Visuals Unlimited/Sylvan H. Wittwer, 28; Archive Photos, 29; North Wind Picture
Archives/Nancy Carter, 30 top; Wyoming Division of Cultural Resources, 30 bottom; courtesy of
the Bancroft Library, University of California, Berkeley, 32; North Wind Picture Archives, 35;
courtesy of the Bancroft Library, University of California, Berkeley, 37; North Wind Picture
Archives/Nancy Carter, 38; Visuals Unlimited/Richard Thom, 41.

Editors: E. Russell Primm and Emily J. Dolbear
Photo Researcher: Svetlana Zhurkina
Photo Selector: Dawn Friedman
Design: Bradfordesign, Inc.
Cartography: XNR Productions, Inc.

Library of Congress Cataloging-in-Publication Data

Blashfield, Jean F.
   The Oregon Trail / by Jean F. Blashfield.
      p. cm. — (We the people)
   Includes bibliographical references and index.
   Summary: An introductory history of the Oregon Trail and its significance in opening the west
to settlers, including information on the people who opened the Trail, their reasons for going west,
modes of transportation, and a description of a typical day on the Trail.
   ISBN 0-7565-0045-1 (lib. bdg.)
   1. Oregon Trail—Juvenile literature. [1. Oregon Trail. 2. Overland journeys to the Pacific.
3. Frontier and pioneer life—West (U.S.)] I. Title. II. We the people (Compass Point Books).
   F597 B595 2000
   978'.02—dc21   00-008674

TABLE OF CONTENTS

HEADING WEST

Adventurous men and women from the young United States wanted to see what lay in the West. They hoped to make new homes and farms and towns out of a wilderness.

In the early years, a huge barrier blocked the way west. The Rocky Mountains sliced through the middle of the continent. The highest mountains—many of them 14,000 feet (4,270 meters) high—formed the **Continental Divide**, which separates the rivers flowing east and west. The rivers on the east of the Divide flow to the Atlantic Ocean. Those on the west flow to the Pacific.

A few Americans had reached the Pacific Ocean. Some were fur trappers and traders.

Pioneers heading west had to travel over the Rocky Mountains.

A fur trapper crossing the mountains

They were willing to face the dangers of crossing the mountains on foot. Others were settlers with enough time and money to travel by ship around South America. But there seemed to be no way for an ordinary family to cross the Continental Divide.

Then, in the 1830s, the barrier was opened. A low place between the mountains, called a **pass**, had been found in 1812. Its discovery opened up a pathway that came to be called the Oregon Trail. Within a few decades, some 300,000 hardy pioneers risked death to reach Oregon Country. Their spirit changed the face of the United States.

A wagon train on the Oregon Trail crosses Wyoming.

OPENING THE TRAIL

In the Louisiana Purchase of 1803, the United States bought land from France. The land extended all the way from the Mississippi River to the Rocky Mountains. Beyond it lay a region called Oregon Country. That region included the land north of California and west of the Continental Divide to the Pacific Ocean.

In 1812, a Scottish fur trader named Robert Stuart was heading east to make the challenging climb through the Rockies. To his amazement, he found himself quickly heading down again, having passed through the mountains almost at a leisurely stroll. By chance, he had found a pass through the Rockies.

Twelve years later, in 1824, mountain men Jim Bridger and Jedediah Smith followed Stuart's route. Over time, that route came to be called South Pass. Then in 1832, Captain Benjamin Bonneville of the U.S. Army made the trip through South

Jim Bridger was a famous mountain man.

Pass with a wheeled cart that carried a cannon. At last, the way seemed to be open for settlers.

A young New England businessman named Nathaniel Wyeth wanted to know more about the possibilities of Oregon Country. In 1832, he joined up

Jedediah Smith

9

with frontiersman William Sublette. They pioneered the route of 1,924 miles (3,096 kilometers) to the Columbia River. It became the Oregon Trail.

Captain Benjamin Bonneville

While there were few white settlers in Oregon Country, many Native Americans lived there. The two biggest fur companies—John Jacob Astor's American Fur Company and the Canadian Hudson's Bay Company—had already built trading posts in the region. By a treaty signed in 1818, Britain and the United States claimed Oregon Country. They agreed that anyone could settle there.

Nathaniel Wyeth

In 1846, a new treaty drew a line between British and U.S. territory at the 49th parallel. The U.S. government created Oregon Territory in 1848. It included what are now the states of Washington, Oregon, and Idaho, along with part of Montana.

Trading posts supplied wagon trains on the Oregon Trail.

THE FIRST MISSIONARIES

Encouraged by Wyeth's success, the Congregational Church's Board of Missions sent **missionaries** to spread religion to Oregon Country. In 1835, pioneers Marcus Whitman and Samuel Parker established a mission among the Nez Perce Indians.

Marcus Whitman was a missionary.

The next year, Whitman—along with his bride, Narcissa, and missionaries Henry and Eliza Spalding—started out from the Missouri River. The missionaries traveled with a group of seventy frontiersmen, some wealthy British sportsmen who wanted to hunt buffalo, and 400 packhorses and mules. The missionaries had two heavy

Christian missionaries on the Oregon Trail taught their religion to the Native Americans.

wagons, fourteen horses, six pack mules, and
seventeen cattle, mostly milk cows.

Whitman refused to listen to the guides, who
told him to leave his large wagons behind. After
reaching the Snake River with great difficulty,

This marker on the Oregon Trail honors the memory of two woman missionaries, Narcissa Whitman and Eliza Spalding.

the disgusted guides abandoned the missionaries. They finally arrived in Oregon without their wagons. However, Narcissa Whitman and Eliza Spalding had become the first European women to cross the Continental Divide. And travelers learned not to travel with such heavy wagons.

In 1843, Marcus Whitman led the first of the big wagon trains along the Oregon Trail. Called the Great Migration, this wagon train included 1,000 people.

In 1847, Whitman's mission, near what is now Walla Walla, Washington, was struck by an outbreak of measles. The Cayuse Indians blamed the settlers for bringing the disease that killed so many Indian children. They attacked the mission, killing the Whitmans and others and kidnapping many women and children.

Despite these tragedies, the Oregon Trail was now open. Over the next twenty-five years, hundreds of thousands of people made the trek, changing the country forever.

WHO WENT, AND WHY?

Travelers on the Oregon Trail faced great hardships. Even after they reached the West, they had a hard life with many challenges. So why did they go?

Back then, Americans were still pioneers. They had always headed west—west from Europe

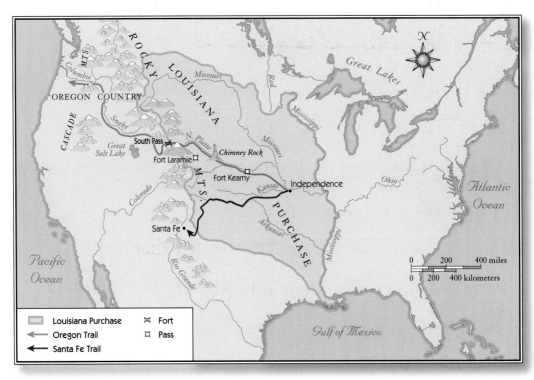

Map of the Oregon Trail

to America, west from the East to the Midwest—searching for greater opportunities. Oregon was the next step west. As author Jonathan Nicholas wrote, "The remarkable odyssey of these [travelers], whose journey comprised one of the largest peacetime migrations in history, was born in the most irresistible of human urges—the search for a fresh start . . . the surge of hope over experience."

Many Americans at that time believed they had the right to all the land that stretched west to the Pacific Ocean. They called this right America's **Manifest Destiny**. They used the idea to justify expansion into western lands that did not belong to the United States. We now know that this belief was unfair. It meant that settlers traveled west and took more and more land from the Native Americans.

THE ALL-IMPORTANT WAGON

A wagon and the animals needed to pull it were important parts of the journey west. The most popular wagon traveling on the Oregon Trail was called a Conestoga wagon. It was named after the place in Pennsylvania where these wagons were first made.

The Conestoga wagon was usually about 10 feet (3 m) long and 4 feet (1 m) wide with sides about 2.5 feet (0.8 m) high. A high, rounded canvas roof made it a covered wagon. With the wheels removed, the wagon could be used as a boat.

Barrels of flour, cornmeal, sugar, and coffee were roped to the sides of the wagon. Smaller items were kept in pockets sewn to the insides

A Conestoga wagon without its familiar white canvas roof

Settlers carried most of their things in their wagons.

of the canvas cover. Trunks and crates filled the wagon. A family had to take enough supplies for at least six months on the trail. They also had to carry the supplies needed to establish a home and farm when the journey was over.

It took at least four oxen or teams of four to six horses to pull a single wagon. One family may have had two or more wagons. Caring for the cattle, as the oxen were called, was a full-time job. Families also traveled with milk cows, horses, mules, goats, sheep, dogs, cats, and chickens.

Traveling the long Oregon Trail required planning.

ON THE TRAIL

Travelers on the Oregon Trail had to plan their journey carefully according to the seasons. They could not leave Missouri until the prairie grasses were high enough for their animals to graze. And they had to cross the Cascade Mountains, which lie parallel to the Pacific Coast, before the winter snows started in November. Timing was critical.

The region around Independence, Missouri, was the jumping-off point for settlers. Here the Missouri River, on which they had traveled up from St. Louis, turns north and can no longer be used for a journey westward.

During the first weeks, the pioneers learned how to drive the wagons, tend the oxen, sleep

Wagon trains had to cross large prairies such as this one.

A dangerous part of the journey was getting wagon trains through rivers.

under the stars, cook over outdoor fires—and
stay cheerful. They also had to learn how to cross
rivers, the most dangerous part of the journey.

The first river they encountered after leaving
Independence was the Big Blue. Its steep banks
often sent wagons skidding down into the water.
Some settlers were drowned there before they had

even left Missouri. Rivers farther west looked safe—they were broad and shallow. But these rivers often had soft sand or even quicksand that could swallow up a heavy wagon.

One of the first things the settlers saw on the Great Plains were buffalo, or **bison**, which numbered in the millions. The pioneers usually didn't know, or didn't care, that Native Americans relied on bison for food and many other needs. Travelers often hunted down the big, shaggy beasts for "fun."

At Fort Kearny, the pioneers entered the green valley of the Platte River. Surrounding them was the awesome Great American Desert, as the Great Plains were then called. Fortunately, they could catch sight of landmarks many miles away.

The first settlers saw bison such as these.

Chimney Rock was a landmark for travelers of the Oregon Trail.

The most memorable landmark was Chimney Rock jutting up from the Plains some miles before Fort Laramie. The rock told the travelers that mountains lay ahead.

From Fort Kearny to South Pass, pioneers on the Oregon Trail often saw other travelers taking the Mormon Trail. Members of the Church of Jesus Christ of Latter-day Saints, or Mormons, had been forced out of their homes

Many Mormon families made the journey west on the Mormon Trail.

in Illinois and Iowa. Starting in 1847, they too headed west toward a land they could call their own—Utah.

The Oregon Trail was busy. On a single day in June 1850, soldiers at Fort Laramie counted

550 wagons passing. At least 2,000 people passed the fort that day. They often put their signatures on rocks along the way. Today, the rock at Register Cliff has names carved into it.

The rock with names carved in it at Register Cliff, Wyoming

Fort Laramie

A Day on the Trail

It took three hours every morning to get ready. The pioneers got up at 4 A.M., blasted from sleep by a trumpet. They ate breakfast, gathered the livestock, harnessed the oxen, and headed out by 7 A.M.

Children as young as four and five years old walked with the older children alongside the wagon. People walked because sitting in a wagon without springs was harder on the body than walking.

After the first few days on the trail, excitement usually died down. Amelia Knight kept a journal of her family's journey, filled with boredom broken by disaster. "We are creeping

Life on the trail

along slowly, one wagon after another, the same old gait; and the same thing over and over, out of one mud hole and into another all day."

At noon, the wagons stopped and the women fixed a cold meal. There might also be a meeting of the wagon train's leaders to decide any issues. But they couldn't stop long. The pioneers tried to travel at least 16 miles (26 km) every day.

In early evening, the wagon-train leader went on ahead to find a good place to stop for the night. First, he marked out a huge circle. Then he marked the spot where each wagon would park. Together, the wagons made a barrier that kept the animals safe for the night.

As soon as the wagon train stopped for the night, the children had to find firewood. If they couldn't find wood, they collected dried buffalo droppings, called buffalo chips. Once dried, the droppings had no smell and burned well. Each family built a fire in a circle of stones. They stood three sticks in a triangle to support a heavy cooking pot. Coffee pots and three-legged frying pans called spiders were placed on the hot stones.

They ate the same foods for dinner as they ate at other meals—beans, bacon, and bread. Any fresh meat or fruit they found was a welcome change. In 1857, pioneer Helen Carpenter recorded in her diary, "How we do wish for some vegetables. I can really scent them cooking sometimes. One does like a change and about the only change we have from bread and bacon is bacon and bread."

Cooking the evening meal

Getting enough water was a problem too. The pioneers had to fill barrels with it whenever they could. Sometimes that water supply had to last a long time. In 1852, a pioneer named W. B. Evans wrote in his diary, "Our drinking water is living . . . that is, it is composed of one-third green fine moss, one-third pollywogs, and one-third embryo mosquitoes . . . [which] we strain through our teeth."

After dinner and cleaning up, it might be time for everyone to join in music or storytelling. People who could play musical instruments took them along, knowing that music would help them through the lonely nights.

The saddest times on the trail were when someone died because of an accident or an illness.

Death was common on the Oregon Trail.

Graves on the Oregon Trail

38

Usually a doctor traveled in a large wagon train, but he could rarely do much to help. The survivors had to dig a grave beside the trail, bury the dead person, and move on.

On the trail, death was a fact of life. It has been estimated that about 10 percent of all pioneers died on the journey. That could be as many as 30,000 people. Although many easterners feared Native Americans, Indians killed fewer than 400 pioneers during the twenty years that settlers traveled the Oregon Trail.

THE END OF THE TRAIL

When the Civil War began in the East in 1861, most easterners gave up any plans to go west. Very few pioneers moved along the trail during the war years. Soon after the war ended, the **transcontinental railroad** was completed. Though the Oregon Trail was used for another twenty years, its place in U.S. history was over.

Sadly, many pioneers who made the terrible journey did not find what they wanted in Oregon. Others, however, claimed land and settled in for the long work of making a better life. These pioneers helped establish the new states—Oregon in 1859, Washington and Montana in 1889, and Idaho and Wyoming in 1890. The trek they made

Ruts caused by heavy wagon wheels on the Oregon Trail are still visible today.

across the country on the Oregon Trail became
part of the heroic legends of American history.

GLOSSARY

bison—buffalo

Continental Divide—a stretch of high ground formed by the crests of the Rocky Mountains. Rivers on the east flow to the Atlantic and rivers on the west flow to the Pacific.

Manifest Destiny—the belief that Americans had the right to all the western land all the way to the Pacific Ocean

missionaries—people who travel to teach religion

pass—a low place in a mountain range

transcontinental railroad—a railway that runs from coast to coast

DID YOU KNOW?

- Traveling the Oregon Trail took at least four months. Completing the trail in five months was considered good time.

- Because their white canvas roofs made the wagons on the Oregon Trail look like ships, they were called prairie schooners.

- So many thousands of pioneers carved their names on Independence Rock that it came to be called Guestbook Rock.

- Some families traveled the Oregon Trail by wagon as late as 1912 because they couldn't afford the train fare.

IMPORTANT DATES

Timeline

1812	Robert Stuart discovers South Pass across the Continental Divide.
1832	The first wheeled vehicle travels through South Pass; Nathaniel Wyeth and William Sublette pioneer the Oregon Trail.
1836	Narcissa Whitman and Eliza Spalding become the first European women to cross the Continental Divide.
1843	The Great Migration, the first big wagon train along the Oregon Trail, takes place.
1846	The Oregon Treaty divides Oregon Country at the 49th parallel. Britain gets the northern part and the United States gets the southern part.
1848	Oregon Territory is created.
1859	Oregon becomes the 33rd state on February 14.
1869	The transcontinental railroad is completed.

IMPORTANT PEOPLE

HENRY SPALDING

(1804–1874), *missionary and pioneer, husband of Eliza Spalding*

MARCUS WHITMAN

(1802–1847), *missionary and pioneer, leader of the Great Migration along the Oregon Trail*

NARCISSA WHITMAN

(?–1847), *missionary and pioneer, and with Eliza Spalding, one of the first European women to cross the Continental Divide*

NATHANIEL WYETH

(1802–1856), *businessman who pioneered the Oregon Trail*

WANT TO KNOW MORE?

At the Library

McNeese, Tim. *Western Wagon Trains.* New York: Crestwood House, 1993.

Nicholas, Jonathan. *On the Oregon Trail.* Portland, Ore.: Graphic Arts
   Center Publishing Company, 1992.

Paulsen, Gary. *Tucket's Gold.* New York: Delacorte Press, 1999.

Steedman, Scott. *A Frontier Fort on the Oregon Trail.* New York: P. Bedrick
   Books, 1993.

Stefoff, Rebecca. *The Oregon Trail in American History.* Springfield, N.J.:
   Enslow, 1997.

On the Web

End of the Oregon Trail Interpretive Center

http://www.teleport.com/~eotic/

For a brief history of the Oregon Trail, including its pioneers and the
wagons and equipment they used

The Oregon Trail

http://www.isu.edu/~trinmich/Oregontrail.html

For facts, trail sites, and information about the people who traveled the
Oregon Trail

People in the West: Marcus and Narcissa Whitman

http://www3.pbs.org/weta/thewest/wpages/wpgs400/w4whitma.htm

For descriptions of the work and tragic death of this missionary couple who
played an important role in opening the Oregon Trail

Through the Mail

Oregon State Archives

800 Summer Street N.E.

Salem, OR 97310

For more information about the people who traveled the Oregon Trail

On the Road

End of the Oregon Trail Interpretive Center

Oregon City, OR 97045

503/657-9336

To visit the end of the Oregon Trail

INDEX

About the Author

Jean F. Blashfield has worked for publishers in Chicago, Illinois, and Washington, D.C. A graduate of the University of Michigan, she has written about ninety books, most of them for young people. Jean F. Blashfield has two college-age children and lives in Delavan, Wisconsin.

NIS